Original title:
The Garden's Gift

Copyright © 2025 Creative Arts Management OÜ
All rights reserved.

Author: Riley Hawthorne
ISBN HARDBACK: 978-1-80567-028-5
ISBN PAPERBACK: 978-1-80567-108-4

Serenity in Petal Form

In the patch where weeds collide,
A dandelion wears a mustache wide.
Bees buzz with gossip, 'What's the dish?'
They sip sweet nectar, granting every wish.

Tulips dance in a breezy waltz,
While roses blush at their own faults.
A sunflower grins at the neighboring crew,
Saying, 'Check out my tan, how about you?'

The Canvas of the Earth

Nature's palette, splashes of green,
Frogs in bow ties hop, so keen.
Crickets tune their orchestral play,
As puppies dig holes, ruining the day.

Mice in the thickets nibble on cheese,
While squirrels arm wrestle, if you please.
In this art blur, oh what a sight,
Every twirl and tumble feels just right.

Hues of Joy and Reflection

The tulip tops wear crazy hats,
While snails in tuxedos strut like brats.
The daisies giggle as wind swirls them,
In this place, who could feel grim?

Marigolds gossip, petals all a-twitch,
As butterflies dance, each one a rich pitch.
A ladybug twirls, a superstar move,
Underneath the sun, they groove and groove.

Blossoms for the Soul's Journey

Eggplants shimmer, beaming like jewels,
Radishes chuckle, they're no fools.
In the patchwork maze where veggies reside,
A cabbage prances with boogie pride.

Petunias' puns make bees laugh aloud,
While tomatoes blushing, feel quite proud.
In this funny realm, bloom after bloom,
Every sprout's laugh dispels all gloom.

Rhythms of the Rain

Pitter-patter, what a sound,
Each drop dances on the ground.
Frogs croak out a silly tune,
As worms twist like they're out of swoon.

Clouds above wear a jaunty grin,
While flowers giggle, soft and thin.
Raindrops play hopscotch with the air,
Splashing puddles without a care.

Seeds of Reflection

What's that sprout peeking through dirt?
A brave little thing, not scared of hurt.
It stretches high, seeking the sun,
While ants below plot a little fun.

A dandelion wishes on a breeze,
"Pick me! You can't, I'm hard to seize!"
But when kids blow, seeds take a flight,
Tickling noses, what a funny sight!

Halos of Hope

A butterfly with polka-dot wings,
Flutters by, and everybody sings.
"I'm a queen," it claims, with a laugh,
But it's just a moth in a puffed-up scarf!

The sun peeks through a fluffy cloud,
Tickling blooms, making them proud.
"Oh dear, look! I've made a bouquet!"
A bee buzzes, "I was just here to play!"

Wreathed in Nature's Charm

Squirrels chase and play tag on trees,
While rabbits nap in the gentle breeze.
A flower giggles, "Look at me sway!"
The bees just buzz, "We'll join the fray!"

A leaf fell down, and what a scene,
It landed right on a grasshopper's green.
"Now I'm a hat!" it claims with glee,
While the critters laugh, "Oh, look at thee!"

Tranquility in Nature's Embrace

In my yard, a squirrel pranced,
He stole my snacks, then danced.
A robin chirps a cheeky tune,
As I reclaim my crumbs at noon.

The daisies giggle in the breeze,
While ants march like they own these trees.
A tortoise slowly takes a peek,
I swear he winked—oh, what a sneak!

A Mosaic of Growth and Renewal

The carrots wear a dirty coat,
As rabbits plot, they slyly gloat.
Tomatoes blush like they got caught,
In a scandalous veggie thought.

The sunshine tickles green old grass,
While beetles dance with flair and sass.
The daisies hold a flower show,
And daisies know they steal the show!

Radiance of the Fluttering Leaves

A butterfly misreads the map,
And lands upon my neighbor's lap.
The winds are giggling, chatting sweet,
While sunflowers sway and tap their feet.

The leaves are laughing, let them be,
They love to play hide and seek with me.
A squirrel's got his acorn stash,
He hides it quick, what a mad dash!

The Breath of Verdant Life

In this patch of greens and grays,
A lettuce sings on sunny days.
The peas hold hands, they're such good friends,
They plot a party that never ends.

The flowers gossip, oh so loud,
As clouds float by, feeling proud.
A bumblebee brings news of cheer,
And buzzes whispers for all to hear!

Harmony in Root and Soil

In leafy lanes, the gnomes do play,
Chasing butterflies throughout the day.
With shovels, they dig and sing a tune,
Laughing at squirrels under the moon.

The worms tell jokes, they wiggle with cheer,
While flowers gossip, their petals so near.
Pumpkins wear hats, quite silly and round,
As carrots dance, in the soft, loamy ground.

Secrets Linger in the Shade

Behind the bushes, whispers unfold,
Where ladybugs share secrets untold.
Bees in their buzz, a funny charade,
As cats hide sly in the cool, leafy shade.

The sunflowers lean, like they're eavesdropping,
While raccoons plan their midnight flopping.
A stolen snack from the picnic spread,
Leaves the poor squirrels scratching their heads.

Whispers of Blossoms

The tulips giggle, their colors so bright,
While daisies whisper of last night's fright.
The roses chuckle, their thorns on display,
Saying, 'Watch out, or you'll dance our way!'

In a corner, the violets plot,
Hatching a scheme for a garden pot.
With laughter and blooms, they twirl in delight,
Creating a show under stars so bright.

Secrets in the Soil

Down in the earth, the secrets prepare,
As roots share tales of what's not quite fair.
The radishes wink from their cozy beds,
While the beetroot grumbles and shakes its reds.

Fungi form circles, they dance and prance,
While tiny critters join in the chance.
A comedy club where the greens take the stage,
In a world where soil is the wisest sage.

Beneath the Canopy

Under leaves that dance and sway,
A squirrel stole my lunch today.
He grinned and dashed up a tree,
Now I'm left with just a pea.

Flowers laugh and wag their tails,
While bees are telling funny tales.
The daisies wink, the roses chat,
With every gaffe, I toss my hat.

A rogue snail slipped and did a twirl,
Saying, "Hey, I'm just a swirl!"
The mushrooms giggle, tip their caps,
In this lush world, we take some naps.

Chasing shadows, tossing jokes,
Among the chattering, cheerful folks.
Each day's a party, come what may,
In the whimsy of nature's play.

Serenade of the Sunlight

Sunlight beams on tangled vines,
Tickling leaves and whispering lines.
A butterfly wears tiny shoes,
It flits around as if it's news.

The ants march in a silly line,
Each one thinks it's just divine.
They bump and giggle, lose their way,
Who knew? Ants could dance and sway!

A shadow darts, oh what a sight,
A cat with dreams of catching light.
He pounces twice, then takes a break,
Turns out, he's just a nap mistake.

Amidst the bloom and giggles wide,
Nature's laughter can't abide.
With every prank that flowers share,
Life echoes back with joyous flair.

Harvest of Dreams

The cornfields whisper jokes at night,
While pumpkins wear their grinning might.
A scarecrow can't quite hold his hat,
Each breeze shakes off the strawling cat.

Zucchinis boast their size and shape,
While radishes, with ribbons drape.
A gopher digs, but finds surprise,
A worm's in there with big, bright eyes.

The tomatoes throw a summer bash,
Dancing 'round with a fancy sash.
They slip and slide on dewy grass,
Who knew they'd form a giggly class?

With every wink from leafy green,
Life's a play, and oh, how keen!
We gather smiles beneath the moon,
This harvest brings a funny tune.

Echoes of Growth

Beneath the sun, the seedlings giggle,
As worms perform their squirmy wiggle.
Roots entwined in tales of clay,
Sway with rhythms of the play.

A broccoli sports a leafy crown,
It parades around the garden town.
The carrots tease in orange cheer,
"We're the best and always near!"

With daisies blowing silly kisses,
The wind joins in, it never misses.
All branches hum a sunny song,
In echoes where the laughs belong.

Each sprout and bud, a comic scene,
In nature's world where fun's routine.
So here beneath the sky so wide,
We dance and laugh, and so abide.

Embers of the Earth

Beneath the dirt, a worm's great dream,
To wiggle and squirm while sipping cream.
It brought a friend, a tiny ant,
Who told a joke that made it chant.

A squirrel with acorns stacked so high,
Declared his stash could reach the sky.
But in his climb, he slipped and rolled,
A leafy plunge, a story bold.

Just then a rabbit popped on through,
In search of greens, he found a shoe.
With one big hop, he missed his mark,
And splashed into a puddle dark.

The sun set low, the critters laughed,
As shadows danced, their worries waft.
In nature's play, with laughter clear,
The silly tales we hold so dear.

Grace of the Greenery

In the lush leaves where secrets play,
A chicken clucks at a grand ballet.
Her feathers fluff, a sight to cheer,
When startled, she leaps, without a fear.

The mushrooms giggle, all in a row,
Sporting hats in the soft light's glow.
They dance in breezes, twirls and spins,
While teasing bugs with tiny grins.

A frog croaks jokes that make trees sway,
While flowers nodding, hear him say,
"Why do we bloom? To show off style!"
With blooms so bright, they can't help smile.

All around, the laughter flows,
In the meadow where mischief grows.
With grace in every silly turn,
Nature's joy is what we yearn.

A Journey Through Shades

A snail on a quest, slow as can be,
Wore a shell like a hat, quite cleverly.
He met a grasshopper, quick in his leaps,
Who challenged him with dizzying peeps.

Together they ventured, zigzag and dart,
Through dappled light, each played their part.
The snail made a trail, bright and slim,
While the hopper sang tunes, bright and grim.

They found a toadstool, wide and stout,
Where critters gathered, all came out.
A lizard cracked jokes that tickled the air,
As each little laugh tangled in hair.

At dusk they returned, tired yet spry,
Underneath stars, they waved goodbye.
A friendship forged on this funny spree,
Through shades of laughter, wild and free.

Sunrise Over Petal Paths

Morning breaks with colors so bold,
Petals wake to tales retold.
A bee with dreams of royal flair,
Got lost in blossom, twirling in air.

A butterfly sneezed, a sight to see,
Sending pollen flying, oh dear me!
It landed right on a sleeping cat,
He woke up shocked, then took a spat.

The sunbeams danced on blades of grass,
As rabbits giggled, they took a pass.
They hopped in circles, a joyful sight,
Turning their morning into delight.

With every bloom, a story spun,
In the petal paths, laughter runs.
So greet the morn with a grinning face,
Nature's wonder, a funny place.

Whispers of Blooming Secrets

In the corner, a gnome gives a wink,
As daisies gossip over lemonade drink.
They spill tales of bees in fancy attire,
While tulips giggle, caught in their lyre.

A dandelion thinks it's a wish come true,
But the yard's just a mess, no one knows what to do.
The roses can't stop their gossiping tease,
While daisies roll over, just aiming to please.

A Tapestry of Green Dreams

The ivy's a climber, with ambitions so grand,
While veggies plot takeovers—oh, isn't it grand?
Cabbages band up with carrots in fright,
As tomatoes throw parties by soft moonlight.

The herbs have a secret, behind the sage's back,
They're planning a rave, perhaps a snack attack.
It's all growing wild, with laughter and cheer,
Nature's own circus, come see the show here!

Petals Embrace the Dawn

As sun creeps in, the tulips all sway,
Woken up early, they dance, come what may.
The lilies are giddy, stretching with glee,
While daisies declare, "Join us for tea!"

The morning is buzzing, with colors so bright,
As crickets hum softly, not ready for flight.
With laughter and petals, the day starts anew,
With jokes in the breeze, and sprinkles of dew.

Nature's Hidden Treasures

Beneath fluffy clouds, the secrets unfurl,
A snail's fashion show—a slimy new pearl!
The ants march in style, with swagger and flair,
While caterpillars gossip with flair in the air.

A berry's brave tale of being a snack,
Results in a debate about red versus black.
With giggles and tinkles, the flora all sing,
Amongst nature's jokes, there's joy in the spring!

Roots of Connection

In the soil where secrets thrive,
Worms wiggle and the carrots jive.
The radishes giggle, the beets just stew,
Because no one can root like this crew!

Underneath the leafy gowns,
Potatoes whisper, playing clowns.
Each spud has jokes, each bulb a pun,
The underground comedy's just begun!

Sunbeams crack through leafy hats,
While veggies trade their silly chats.
Corn leans over, ears a-flutter,
'Kernels of wisdom,' says the butter!

But when the rain comes pouring down,
Beets hold tight, don't dare to frown.
They stomp and dance in muddy glee,
'Let's throw a splash party, just you and me!'

The Dance of the Pollinators

Buzzing and flapping, what a sight,
Bees gather round, in sheer delight.
A butterfly twirls, oh what finesse,
Sipping sweet nectar in its best dress.

Ladybugs cheer with a tiny clap,
As flies do tumbles, a constant hap.
The flowers sway to this buzzing tune,
It's a wild rave, by light of the moon.

Moths join in, with their disco moves,
Pollination grooves that make you groove.
'Pollinators unite, let's share the fun,
A garden soirée, for everyone!'

But watch your step, oh where you tread,
A dancing bee just bumped its head.
'Accidental tango!' it buzzes in rhyme,
In this garden, every step's prime time!

Sun-Kissed Serenity

Basking in warmth, the daisies yawn,
While sunflowers proudly wave at dawn.
With a wink of pollen, they take a peek,
At bumblebees dancing, oh so unique!

The zucchini struts, with swagger and zest,
'Look at my blossoms, aren't they the best?'
While tomatoes roll their little red eyes,
'They've got garden flair, but we have pies!'

Nearby, a gopher tries to play cool,
Digging and digging, breaking the rule.
His nose knows best, a treasure to find,
Yet he leaves chaos, oh so unkind!

But laughter echoes from leafy retreats,
As veggies debate on their cute little feats.
'Who wore it best, the carrot or pea?'
'In your dreams,' they say, 'it's clearly just me!'

Hidden Treasures of the Earth

Digging down deep, what do we see?
Old boots, a spoon, and maybe a bee!
'Treasure hunting is quite the feat,
When all you find is last week's sweet beet!'

The potatoes chuckle, as roots intertwine,
'Finding old toys, guess they're divine!'
While onions cry over past memories,
'Just don't peel too deep, it's bound to freeze!'

A rusty old bucket, a garden's delight,
Whispers of stories in the soft moonlight.
'Just think of the secrets we've hidden away,
A pirate's bounty? No, just yesterday's hay!'

Yet laughter erupts from each raucous search,
For weeds wear crowns like a funky church.
'Call all the critters, it's time to play,
In our treasure trove, there's fun every day!'

Echoing Stillness

In the green, where daisies dance,
A squirrel prances, what a chance!
He slips and slides, oh what a sight,
Chasing his tail in sheer delight.

The tulips whisper, 'Do not fall,'
While butterflies, they laugh and call.
A snail rolls by, so slow, so meek,
With garden gossip, so to speak.

A gnome looks on with painted grin,
As frogs perform, a leap within.
With every hop, the daisies sway,
Oh silly joys of summer's play!

Yet when the night begins to creep,
The critters know it's time for sleep.
But who would think a snore could be,
The loudest sound in greenery?

Odes to Blooming

With blooms that boast in colors bright,
The peonies dressed, a lovely sight.
They prance around like fancy folks,
While nearby, laughing, are the croaks.

A band of bees in striped attire,
Buzzing tunes like a quirky choir.
They bump and jiggle, what a fuss,
Trying to dance, but missing thus!

And lilies sway with gentle charm,
While petals droop, they mean no harm.
"Oh, the sun is far too strong!"
They sing and swing, all day long.

In every corner, laughter flows,
As sprouts make jokes with budding prose.
Each whimsy laughs with fragrant cheer,
The blooms unite, our giggly sphere.

Beneath the Verdant Veil

Beneath the leaves, the critters tease,
A rabbit hops with utmost ease.
"Catch me if you can!" he squeals,
Past dancing ferns and wobbly meals.

The carrots chuckle, 'We're so fine!'
While cabbage rolls in leafy line.
"Let's hide and seek, it's so much fun!"
As veggies melt beneath the sun.

But when the moon begins to glow,
The nighttime blooms put on a show.
The flowers yawn and share their pranks,
As crickets join, with laughs and thanks.

In gardens lush where joy runs rife,
The blooms remind us: love is life.
Each petal shares, with cheeky thrill,
The joy of nature, laughter's will!

A Legacy of Leaves

In autumn's breeze, the leaves conspire,
Each tumble tells of a backyard choir.
Squirrels gather for a nutty feast,
Even worms are shaking like a dancing beast.

With colors bright, they flap and glide,
While I chase them, oh, what a ride!
A leaf slipped past, it gave a wink,
Guess it's true, even leaves can think.

They plan escape from the messy lawn,
With every gust, they twirl and brawn.
As I rake them into a pile so tall,
They conspire to dance — oh, what a brawl!

So next time you stroll through nature's hall,
Remember the leaves, with their sneaky call.
They leave behind laughter, a comedy scripted,
In every crumple, wisdom is gifted.

Silence Between the Petals

In the flowers' talk, who'd have guessed,
They gossip softly while we all rest.
A daisy said, 'I'm quite the charmer!'
While tulips roll eyes, 'Oh, what a farmer!'

The roses boast of their lovely smell,
But bees chime in, 'It's a savory spell!'
In whispers of hue, the petals collide,
Hilarity blooms when the sun starts to bide.

With colors galore, they swap their tales,
Of sunlit daydreams and raindrop fails.
Oh, what a hoot when the daisies sway,
They say, 'New shoes won't fit in this play!'

So lean in closer, don't just admire,
The secrets they keep can spark a fire.
In stillness, among the colors that twirl,
Listen for laughter in this colorful whirl.

Mirth in the Meadow

In the meadow's heart, the daisies pop,
They jest about who'll win the hop.
Bouncing around, while bumblebees fail,
Saying, 'Buzz it out, you're far too frail!'

A rabbit winks, with a carrot in tow,
'You might be flowers, but I steal the show!'
With playful nudges and breeze on their skin,
The meadow's a riot, let the fun begin!

The clovers chuckle, intertwined tight,
'I dare you to hop as high as a kite!'
When willows sway, they all stand in awe,
As crickets join in with a comedic draw.

So frolic along, let laughter ignite,
In the meadow of mirth, everything's light.
Life's little antics will capture your gaze,
In the greenest of fields, let joy set ablaze.

Cherished Roots

In the depths of earth, where secrets lie,
Roots tell tales in whispers, oh my!
One said to another, 'Did you hear the news?
A flower got pruned — what did he choose?'

They chuckle at weeds, who shoot up like rockets,
While rabbits dig in their garden pockets.
'You think you're tough, growing wild and free?
Wait till the lawnmower comes after thee!'

And yet beneath, there's love that connects,
Their friendship blooms in quirky respects.
Through storms and sun, they're always entwined,
In giggles galore, mischief defined.

So tiptoe with care, as you stroll along,
For those hidden roots compose a sweet song.
In the thrumming earth, laughter's distinct,
In the life of the garden, it's more than you think.

A Symphony in Full Bloom

The daisies dance with glee,
While tulips hold a tea party.
Bees buzz like a radio,
Sipping nectar like a pro.

Sunflowers play the tallest game,
Challenging the clouds to fame.
Petunias joking, planting seeds,
Whispering to the shyest weeds.

Daffodils wear silly hats,
Cheering up the sleepy brats.
Even roses crack a smile,
Blooming brightly all the while.

But what of thorns, you may ask?
They're the punchline of this task.
Making all of nature laugh,
In this quirky floral half.

The Secret Life of Thorns

Thorns wear glasses, think they're cool,
Pretending they're the classroom fool.
With each prick, they share a joke,
Leaving flowers in a poke.

Roses sigh, "Oh not again!"
While thorns practice their zen.
Buds giggle at their prickly friend,
Saying, "Just don't poke and bend!"

They argue over who's the best,
"I'm so tough, I pass the test!"
Yet, in truth, they all agree,
Without them, life's a mystery.

At night, they dance in silent pacts,
Worried about a garden fax.
"Did we frighten off the bees?"
"Oh look, a dandelion, say cheese!"

Nectar of Untold Stories

In flowers, whispers bloom with zest,
Each with tales they love the best.
Bees with tiny ears, they listen,
As petals gently sway and glisten.

Lavender winks, "I'm quite the saint,
With scent so sweet, I need a paint.
But violets tease me, quite misled,
Their jokes are sharp, they fill with dread."

Sunset hues share tales of gold,
While marigolds are feeling bold.
"Did you hear? The rain gave us a show,
Let's raise a glass to the garden's flow!"

As night descends, they giggle light,
Dreaming of the stars so bright.
In every bloom, a story stays,
A whimsical life in sunny rays.

Serenity Among the Flora

In the quiet corner, mossy green,
Where laughter hides and giggles glean.
Bumbles swing in calm delight,
While crickets chirp through the night.

Ferns tell tales of windy fights,
Against the breeze, reaching new heights.
"Who won?" asks thyme with a smile,
"I did, obviously, by a mile!"

Lilies float like little boats,
While frogs sing silly, sleepy notes.
Grasshoppers dance, their legs in sync,
All wondering what flowers think.

But in this peace, a racket grows,
As daisies shout, "Look at my toes!"
Quiet now, there's joy in play,
In the flora's fun, all's okay!

Blossom's Silent Song

In a patch of green so bright,
A daisy danced, what a sight!
She swayed and spun with glee,
While a snail shouted, "Look at me!"

The bees all giggled, buzzed around,
With petals stacked, they formed a mound.
A squirrel dropped an acorn ball,
And tripped, tumbling, oh what a fall!

A butterfly slipped on fragrant dew,
And wondered, "What's this crazy view?"
With flowers laughing, joy held tight,
In the field, a comical sight!

So if you need a laugh or cheer,
Just find the blooms, they're always near.
They'll share a joke, a funny rhyme,
And make you smile, oh, every time!

The Voyage of Seedlings

Tiny seeds with dreams to grow,
Set sail on winds, to and fro.
Kernels giggle, sprouting bold,
In rowboats made from leaves of gold.

A ladybug, captain so spry,
Turns her ship with a cheerful cry.
"Ahoy! Let's dance upon the breeze!"
While grasshoppers play 'Jump the Leaves!'

But a storm brews, oh, what a fuss!
One seed shouts, "I'm not in the bus!"
They'll float and bob, on waves of rain,
Creating a splash, oh, what a gain!

With each new sprout the laughter grows,
In this green voyage as joy overflows.
They share tall tales of wild seas,
And dream of being tall as trees!

Sunlit Reflections

Beneath the sun, the flowers grin,
As fluffy clouds all swirl and spin.
A sunflower's hat tip, a wink,
Crowds gather 'round, they're on the brink!

A puddle laughs with jiggly fish,
"Come play with me, fulfill a wish!"
A frog jumps up to steal the show,
With tiny leaps, he steals the glow.

"Reflect on this!" the shadows quip,
As dragonflies perform a flip.
Roots poke out, and giggles blend,
Nature's humor has no end!

So when the sun begins to fade,
Know laughter in the light has made
Each petal laugh, each leaf a friend,
In this bright place where smiles ascend!

Nature's Caress

In a meadow where butterflies play,
The flowers shout, "It's a sunny day!"
A bumblebee, with a ruffled wing,
Sings, "I'm here for the sweet, sweet bling!"

The moss waves hello, soft and green,
As ants parade, proud and clean.
"March with us, we're on a quest!"
"Join our game! It's the very best!"

But who knew plants could tell such tales?
Of silly leaves in windy gales?
With laughter caught in every breeze,
They tickle toes and tease the trees!

So when you stroll through nature's place,
Remember smiles are all around space.
From flowers' whimsy to rocks' soft jest,
In every nook, life's humor rests!

The Poetry of Pollination

Bees buzzing round with a clumsy dance,
Pollen flying, giving flowers a chance.
They bumble and tumble, not caring a wit,
Nature's comedy, oh, how they fit!

With nectar on lips like sticky sweet glue,
They flirt with the blooms, it's a wild adieu.
In the sunshine, they share quite the laugh,
Making honey with each little gaffe.

The ants sit nearby with a gossiping stare,
Watching the buzzers have fun in the air.
"Oh look," they chime, "there goes a bee!
That's the worst dance I ever did see!"

Yet without their folly, there'd be no delight,
In fruits and flowers, the colors so bright.
So raise a toast to those bees on the wing,
For all of the laughter and joy that they bring!

A Palette of Seasons

In spring, the flowers throw a colorful show,
Dancing with joy in a fine, breezy blow.
The tulips are gossiping, making a scene,
While daisies are busy with the latest routine.

Summer rolls in, and the sun gets too bold,
Plants wear their shades, oh, the stories unfold!
"Is it hot in here?" the sunflowers sigh,
While buttercups giggle, "We're all feeling spry!"

Then autumn arrives, with a crispy, brown crunch,
Leaves start to tumble, it's a cheerful brunch.
Pumpkins are jokes in their orange attire,
Making us laugh with their round, roguish fire!

Winter brings snows that blanket the scene,
Where snowmen look silly, so plump, and so keen.
"Let's grab a hot cocoa and dance with delight,"
Says the garden so proud of its colorful night!

Where Wildflowers Weep

In fields where wildflowers sway to and fro,
Some droop their heads low, like they're feeling so-so.
"Oh dear," one says, "Is it raining today?"
"Or just the clouds teasing, come out to play?"

The daisies all chuckle, "Don't drown in your tears,
We've got sunny days and some colorful cheers!"
But tulips just giggle, "We look like a mess,
Let's flaunt our idiocy, that's our finesse!"

"It's a wildflower party!" the poppies all shout,
"We'll dance through the drizzle, laugh and walk about!"
With petals a'flutter and joy in the air,
They embrace every droplet, without a care!

So when life feels heavy, just look to the field,
Where nature's absurdity always can yield.
For laughter grows bright where the wildflowers weep,
A reminder to smile, and your sorrows to keep!

Harmony in the Hedges

In the hedges so green, there's a chatter so bright,
Where rabbits debate if to nibble or bite.
"Let's munch on some carrots!" one cheeky hare grins,
While hedgehogs roll by, with their spiky, sly spins.

The squirrels throw acorns like little cannonballs,
Bickering boldly about who hits walls.
"Oh no! Not on my head!" the wise owl declares,
As he ducks and he dodges with sophisticated flares.

Tangled up flowers compete for the crown,
All bursting with laughter, no sign of a frown.
"It's just a friendly battle, who has the best hue?"
Chirps a thrush in the tree, "Come join in our crew!"

In the hedges of joy, the wild antics unfold,
Where nature is laughing, its stories retold.
So come lend an ear to the antics and glee,
For life in the hedges is silly and free!

The Secret Life of a Blossom

In the corner, a tulip sneezed,
Laughed so hard, the daisies teezed.
"I'll dance like stars," the petunias swore,
While the pansies played peekaboo at the door.

Cucumbers wearing sunglasses bright,
Chat about dreams under the moonlight.
A carrot claims it's a superstar,
"Wait till you see my next bazaar!"

But roses just blushed, feeling so shy,
While the sunflowers winked up high.
Every seed has its funny flair,
Even weeds grin without a care!

Life in bloom can be quite the show,
When the radishes start to put on a glow.
Each petal, a story waiting to spin,
In a world where laughter's always in.

Nature's Silent Cures

A worm wore glasses, couldn't see straight,
Said, "These petals might be my fate!"
Butterflies chuckled, flapping with glee,
"Don't worry, dear worm, you're still free!"

A squirrel in boots did pirouettes,
Dropping acorns like confetti sets.
"I'll plant these here, just watch me dash,"
While the ferns snickered, "What a crash!"

A bee in a hat said, "Buzz off, folks,
I'm on a mission; let's crack some jokes!"
The sun chuckled, casting bright light,
As all the critters danced through the night.

In the foliage, secrets intertwine,
With laughter and joy, all is just fine.
Nature giggles in the soft breeze,
With whispers of magic among the trees.

Sunlit Soliloquy

On a sunny day, the daisies debated,
"What if we wore shoes, like we're elated?"
A ladybug laughed, saying, "Not for me!
I prefer my little polka-dot spree!"

Sunflowers tall, heads held aloof,
Claimed they're the ones that raised the roof.
"With this sun, we're rock stars, you see?
Just look at that shade, we'll sip our tea!"

A beetle in shades tried to act cool,
While the grasshoppers danced, breaking the rule.
"Let's throw a party, it's all in good fun,
We'll boogie all day 'til the day is done!"

So humor blooms where sunlight spills,
Where laughter and whimsy dance through the hills.
In this garden of jest, we all unite,
Creating joy in the warm sunlight.

Gardening in Reverie

A gnome with a hat was caught in a dream,
Barking at clouds, or so it did seem.
Garden statues chuckled in place,
"It's just a classic gnome's silly chase!"

The radishes joined in a waltz of delight,
While tulips held hands in the soft twilight.
"I dare you to sprout; let's make a big fuss!"
The zinnias cheered, "Oh, we can't miss that bus!"

The moon peeked down, trying to fit,
Drawing smiles on petals, just a little bit.
Crickets tuned in with a song so spry,
While the beans played the bass, oh my, oh my!

From seeds of laughter, bright dreams do grow,
In this garden of whimsy, joy steals the show.
We cultivate giggles with each passing day,
In this teasing tale where plants laugh and play.

A Tapestry of Colors

In the patch of greens and reds,
A tomato dreamed of becoming bread.
Carrots danced with a funky beat,
While lettuce twirled on its leafy feet.

In this lively patch, the flowers pranced,
Petunias giggling, the daisies danced.
A sillier sight, you'd seldom find,
As petals blew kisses to a bee so blind.

The marigolds wore hats quite tall,
While sunflowers giggled and tried to sprawl.
In this odd gathering, all was bright,
Where veggies and blooms laughed out of sight.

So if you wander past this plot,
Remember it's fun where the seeds are hot!
With nature's humor to keep us spry,
Join the laughter, let it fly high!

From Seed to Song

A tiny seed popped with a shout,
"I'm growing up, no doubt about!"
It sprouted roots and reached for the sun,
While worms below said, "Let's have fun!"

A sunflower winked and blew a tune,
As peas climbed high, chasing the moon.
The radish rapped with a funky rhyme,
While nature's chorus sang in time.

The beans jumped high, trying to sway,
While cabbages giggled at their ballet.
As petals tapped and leaves did sway,
Nature's concert was on display.

So when you're down, plant a seed,
You'll find a laugh is what you need.
With joy in rows and songs that hum,
Step into fun, let laughter come!

The Language of Leaves

Leaves whisper secrets, oh so sly,
"Did you hear the news? The tulips are shy!"
While oaks chuckle at squirrels in chase,
Hiding acorns with hilarious grace.

The ferns gossip, their fronds all a-flutter,
"Did you see that beetle slip in the butter?"
As vines cracked jokes and blossoms burst out,
Nature's language filled the air with a shout!

The daisies nod, sharing a pun,
"Why don't trees use the internet? It's no fun!"
The leaves all laughed, their laughter so clear,
In this vibrant world, there's no need to fear.

So when you stroll through nature's embrace,
Listen closely; it's a comical place.
With each gentle rustle, you'll surely hear,
The jokes of the leaves, bringing good cheer!

Twilight's Fragrance

As the sun dips low, blossoms commence,
Budding laughter fills the air, so dense.
Lilies are giggling, with scents they weave,
Tickling the noses of those who believe.

A daisy grinned at a slumbering bug,
"Wake up, sleepyhead, time for a hug!"
Petals twinkled under the moon's soft glance,
Inviting all critters to join in the dance.

The nightshade whispered, "Roses, beware!
I'm the cutest flower, with secrets to share!"
With fragrances swirling, a perfume so sly,
The nighttime blooms laughed under the sky.

So when twilight falls and all seems surreal,
Remember the humor that blossoms reveal.
In the night's soft whisper, take in the zest,
In scents and in laughter, we're truly blessed!

A Symphony in Full Bloom

In a plot where daisies dance and sway,
A rabbit stole my carrots—hip hooray!
The sun's a joker, playing hide and seek,
While butterflies wear hats—oh, what a clique!

The roses gossip, petals all a-flutter,
'Pointy thorns! Avoid the muddy gutter!'
A bumblebee serenades near the vine,
Bees in tuxedos sip on sweet sunshine.

Lettuce claims its throne, green and so proud,
While crickets croak a tune—quite loud!
The garden's a circus, laughter rings so true,
A merry band of plants, just for you!

Amidst the chaos, laughter blooms bright,
Flora's fantastic, in pure delight!
Each tree waves hello, with branches wide,
In this silly haven, where joy can't hide!

Nature's Gentle Offering

A squirrel swipes my sandwich without a care,
While flowers chuckle, swaying in the air.
The sun's a shining prankster, smiling wide,
As mushrooms sport tiny hats—their source of pride!

Bees buzzing zany, strut like they're cool,
While ladybugs debate the best garden rule.
A gust of wind sends petals high and low,
The tulips all giggle at this fabulous show!

The grass plays hide and seek with the ants,
While pumpkins prance, dreaming of their chance.
Each leaf is a whisper, sharing secrets neat,
In this funny patch of life, nothing's discreet!

Among all the chatter, joy sprinkles the air,
Nature's a jester—laughter everywhere!
With each silly moment and whimsical twist,
The earth's little secrets are things not to miss!

Fables of Flora

In the cozy crook of the old willow tree,
Frogs boast of their jumps and sip chamomile tea.
The daisies throw parties, quite a sight to behold,
While sunflowers gossip, sharing tales bold!

Old oak stands strong, a wise fellow for sure,
'Why do you think bees insist on allure?'
The ferns sway with laughter, always in style,
Mushrooms don shades to remind us of guile.

The sky laughs with clouds, fluffy and bright,
Tickling the wind in an airy delight.
Caterpillars debate who's the best dancer,
Each twist and turn incites a new chancer!

The petals are storytellers, each with a flair,
Crafting fables of fun in the lavender air.
So gather around, take a seat, take a breath,
For in this wild plot, joy dances with zest!

The Heart's Refuge

Here in this patch of whimsy and cheer,
The bunnies are teasing, 'Hey, look over here!'
A squirrel on a branch cracked a bright little joke,
While lilies nod along, in laughter they soak.

The butterflies flit, spreading tales of delight,
As the grass offers tickles, from morning till night.
The daisies chatter, their petals in bloom,
Whispering secrets that chase away gloom!

Ants march in line, proud of their haul,
While the hedgehog giggles—he's short but not small.
Dreamy clouds drift, wearing silly hats,
As the ivy keeps dancing, blending in chats!

Amidst all this joy, the trees gently sway,
In a haven of laughter, come join the play.
With every quiet chuckle and shenanigan bright,
This home made of whimsy is pure delight!

The Abode of Butterfly Dreams

In a field of blooms so bright,
Butterflies dance like they're in flight.
One tripped over a daisy's stem,
'I swear this flower's a wicked gem!'

A ladybug dressed in red couture,
Claimed the petals were a fashion lure.
The bumblebee buzzed with a grin,
'You think you're cute? I'm here to win!'

The ants threw a party on the grass,
With crumbs that came from a kid's lunch pass.
They debated if crumbs tasted sweet,
While dodging creatures with six-legged feet!

At sunset, they giggled under the sky,
Dreaming of cookies and a grand pie.
Nature's jester, oh what a sight,
Making us laugh till we see the night!

Jewel Tones of the Earth

In colors so bright, the petals gleam,
The flowers conspired to start a theme.
'Let's throw a party!' the tulips exclaimed,
'With all of us here, it can't be tamed!'

The violets giggled in purple delight,
'We'll outshine the daisies; hold on tight!'
While sunflowers stretched to catch the sun,
'Our game of hide-and-seek has begun!'

A daffodil chimed in with flair,
'With our charm, they'll all stop and stare!'
But a sunset came with a sleepy yawn,
'Okay, my friends, the fun's nearly gone.'

Oh, to be flowers in glorious hues,
Living our lives with laughter and views.
Nature's own jesters, we flourish and play,
In this mystical world, come what may!

A Bouquet of Time

A quirky bouquet danced on the breeze,
Consisting of plants that loved to tease.
Rose claimed she was the queen of the show,
While Thyme whispered, 'Just go with the flow!'

'I'm the star and everyone knows!'
Clashed the cosmos of daffodils' prose.
They bickered and bantered in fragrant delight,
'Your scent's too strong! Mine is just right!'

Lavender chuckled, so calm and bright,
'When will you two learn? Just feel the light!'
'I'm blooming but humble,' chimed sweet little Sage,
'Join in the fun, let's turn the page!'

Together they laughed, a whimsical sight,
Their petals unfurling in pure delight.
For in this bouquet's colorful rhymes,
They sculpt a masterpiece of silly times!

The Enchantment of Eden

In a shady nook where the critters chat,
A squirrel named Nutty wore a big hat.
'It's my new style, do you like it, friends?'
A fashion debate that never ends!

A crafty raccoon joined the jest,
'You look like the king of a furry fest!'
With acorns as jewels, oh what a sight,
Their laughter rang through the warm twilight.

The hedgehogs rolled with a giggle and spin,
Claiming they were the twirl team to win!
They pranced and they posed all around the glen,
With style that bested their woodland kin.

As the moon rose high, the antics took flight,
They pranced and they danced, a raucous delight.
In the realm of nature, the humor is clear,
With vibrant spirits, they spread joyful cheer!

Echoes of Nature's Bounty

Beneath the sun, the veggies grin,
A carrot jokes, "I'm all in!"
Tomatoes circle, have their say,
"We're juicier than any ol' parfait!"

Insects chatter, buzzing bright,
"Is it just me, or is it flight?"
A caterpillar claims with glee,
"Just wait, dudes, I'll be a butterfly, you'll see!"

Raindrops tap a funny song,
"Come join the fun, you can't go wrong!"
The daisies giggle, swaying low,
"Let's start a dance; oh, let's go!"

Worms in soil, a squirmy crew,
"Watch it now, I'm high in view!"
A gopher peeks, adorned with flair,
"Hide your snacks, I'm almost there!"

The Dance of Seasonal Change

Spring hops in, with rabbit flair,
"New blooms! New friends! Impeccable hair!"
Dandelions tease, they spread so wide,
"Who knew the breeze was on our side?"

Summer struts in, all sun-kissed bright,
"Bees buzzing here? Oh what a sight!"
Picnics call, with lemonade sips,
Laughter spills from picnic chips.

Fall arrives, leaves swirling down,
"We're dressed to impress, no reason to frown!"
Pumpkins grinning, playful gleam,
"Who's ready for pie? It's our big dream!"

Winter winks, with snowflakes spun,
"Let's build a snowman, just for fun!"
Squirrels slip, and the birds sing low,
"Spring will be back, you just wait, you know!"

An Enchanted Pathway

Through winding paths, where laughter flows,
Giggling flowers strike silly poses,
A squirrel with shades, looking so fly,
"Step back, world, I'm ready to try!"

Mushrooms chat, beneath the green,
"Did you hear what the breeze just seen?"
A wise old tree, with tales untold,
"Ever heard the one about the mold?"

Butterflies flit, with colors so bright,
"Catch me if you can, it's pure delight!"
Crickets chirp a jazzy tune,
"Dance with us, beneath the moon!"

A frog leaps high, with a loud croak,
"Let's start a band, just one more joke!"
With each twist and turn, giggles are found,
In every nook, magic abounds!

Blooms of Resilience

Out pops a flower, unafraid to grow,
"Life's full of light, come steal the show!"
Roses puff up, in finest attire,
"Who needs thorns? We're never tired!"

A daisy chuckles, "I might be small,
But watch me stand, I'll never fall!"
In shadows where sunlight may flee,
"They call me weed, but I'm fancy, see?"

If storms come to dance, we'll spin right back,
"Let's strut our petals, and not lose track!"
A sunflower grins, so tall and proud,
"Look at us shine, we've drawn a crowd!"

With every drop, there's humor to find,
"Grow with joy, leave worries behind!"
Nature's laughter fills every square,
In blooms of resilience, we've a flair!

Ephemeral Wonders

In the dirt, a worm finds cheer,
Dancing round without a fear.
His wiggle moves like a grand ballet,
While ladybugs cheer him, 'Hip, hip, hooray!'

Sunflowers glance, oh what a sight,
As bees zoom in, with all their might.
They miss the target and land with a thud,
Cursing the pollen, then covered in mud!

A clumsy frog leaps, in for a snack,
Hoping for flies, but he's off track.
He lands in a pot of fragrant thyme,
Now he thinks he's a herb, oh what a crime!

The daisies giggle, their petals a-flutter,
"Is that a frog, or some garden butter?"
The moon, it chuckles, high up above,
In this little patch of animated love!

Blossoms and Whispers

A tulip shouts, 'I'm tall and proud!'
Whereas a tiny sprout hides in the crowd.
'Will I get a chance to bloom like you?'
The tulip laughs, 'Maybe, if you grew!'

Bees buzz in, a rambunctious crew,
One bumps a rose—oh what a stew!
'Sorry!' they hum, while covered in dew,
'This blossom's sweet! Let's team up anew!'

A toad hops by, thinks he's quite slick,
But lands on a petal—oops, that was quick!
'Oh dear,' he croaks, 'I better scoot!'
While daisies laugh, 'You make a great brute!'

With colors bright, the flowers dance,
Sharing secrets in a wild prance.
Nature's stage, a circus affair,
In this blooming world, there's laughter to spare!

Flourishing Tales

Once a seed said, 'I'll see the sun!'
'But first,' said the soil, 'you must have fun!'
A worm popped up, with a hat made of leaves,
'Let's twist and shout, then plant your dreams!'

Crickets chirp in a rhythm divine,
While petals flutter, feeling just fine.
A butterfly winks, with a flick of her wing,
'Let's throw a ball—let the garden sing!'

The roses blush, their petals will paint,
While the lilacs joke, 'We're fragrant, not faint!'
'Let's brew some nectar,' the bees all agree,
'And toast to the laughter—just you wait and see!'

A mischief of blossoms, a jolly onlooker,
Claiming the day—oh, what a crooker!
From sunup to down, their joy's never stale,
In this patch of life, we flourish, not fail!

Canvas of the Seasons

Spring winks in, with a jolly hop,
Flowers rise up, saying, 'Don't stop!'
A squirrel performs, acrobatic and bold,
Stealing a nut, but a tale to be told.

Summer brings heat, and the garden is laughing,
Plants all gossip, there's no time for slacking.
A grasshopper plays tunes, legs moving with glee,
While ants all tap dance, in perfect esprit!

Autumn arrives, with hues of surprise,
Pumpkins are grinning, in funny disguise.
The leaves swirl around, performing a show,
While a rabbit hops in, just stealing the show!

Winter wraps up, with a frosty retreat,
A snowman moves in, to his own little beat.
'Where's my carrot?' he shouts, feeling quite lost,
While giggles erupt—oh the garden at cost!

Enchanted By Growth

In a patch of green, where veggies collide,
Cucumbers whisper, with secrets they hide.
Tomatoes giggle in the summer's heat,
While carrots plot sneaky things with their feet.

The peas are quite proud, they climb to the sky,
While radishes dance, oh my, oh my!
Zucchini wears hats made of leaves and of sun,
A fashion show, growing green and for fun.

Bumblebees buzz with a tickle and tease,
While ladybugs giggle, eating their cheese.
A kale salad dreams of a party for two,
With dressing and croutons, oh what do we do?

In this quirky plot, where laughter takes root,
Even the garlic is starting to hoot.
Nature's own jesters, with seeds all around,
In the world's wild garden, joy can be found.

Lush Chronicles

Once a sprout thought it could grow tall and wide,
While sharing a tale with its sunflower bride.
'Your petals so bright, they shine like my dreams!'
'Oh darling,' she laughed, 'it's more than it seems!'

The squash rolled around, with such glee in its heart,
Swapping old stories, each one a fine art.
'What's green and can wiggle?' the eggplant did say,
'An old cucumber on a very bad day!'

As carrots exchanged jokes about digging down deep,
The onions cried laughter, or maybe they weep.
Each leaf brought a giggle, each stem had a jest,
In this lush patch, there's no room for rest.

So join in the fun as the daisies all prance,
With dreams in the air, let's all take a chance.
Lush tales from the soil, a carnival sight,
United in laughter, from morning to night.

Secrets of the Sun

Under rays of gold, where shadows play hide,
A mushroom claims wisdom, all sprightly with pride.
'The sun tickles my cap, what a fine little game!'
While gnomes stretch and yawn, feeling quite the same.

Busy bees in a chatter, buzzing tales of delight,
Trading sweet secrets beneath skies so bright.
'We dance every morning on petals so sweet,'
While the tulips are blushing from their little heat.

The daisies exchange secrets they swore were true,
Like how lilies can giggle when rain starts to dew.
A sage by the fence, full of stories galore,
Calls out, 'Hey, did you hear? There's gossip in store!'

So sip with the sun, let laughter run wild,
In this patch of sunshine, we're happiness styled.
With whispers of joy and a sprinkle of jest,
In the realm of the sun, each moment's a fest.

In the Shadow of Vines

In the shadows of green, the critters all chat,
The raccoons tell stories while wearing a hat.
'What's round, juicy, and has a bright hue?'
'An orange in disguise, pretending to be blue!'

The vines twirl and dance, they can't help but tease,
'We'll tangle your shoes, if you please, if you please!'
With chortles of laughter from ferns all around,
In their leafy convention, hilarity found.

A liaison of roots with dreams far and wide,
Spill secrets between them, no reason to hide.
Little bugs are plotting a vegetable feast,
While spinach plays rough-and-tumble, the beast!

As night draws its curtain on this vine-wrapped play,
The whispers grow soft, but the joy will not sway.
So dip in the shadows, with all that you've got,
In a world full of whimsy, let laughter be sought.

Where Roots Dance and Sing

In a soil of giggles, they twist and they twirl,
Roots jive and wiggle, in a botanical whirl.
Worms wear their top hats, in the earth's lively show,
Mice on maracas, with seeds in a row.

Petunias sport spectacles, they can hardly see,
While daisies do cartwheels, quite joyfully.
A snail plays the banjo, with a soft shell strum,
As butterflies high-five, saying, "Here we come!"

The sunbeams chuckle, tickling the leaves,
While plants tell tall tales, oh what a reprieve!
With ladybugs dancing in their polka dot shoes,
Each bloom spreads laughter, like a colorful muse.

As dusk takes a bow, crickets join the band,
Night joins the party, it's all quite unplanned.
While roots keep on dancing, let laughter take wing,
In this patch of pure joy, how the flowers sing!

Fragrant Promises at Twilight

As twilight arrives with a wink and a sigh,
The garden is bustling, oh my, oh my!
Roses wear perfume, too grand to conceal,
While violets whisper, their secrets reveal.

A garden gnome trips, with his nose in the air,
He stumbles on daisies, without any care.
The moon, like a jester, adds sparkle to night,
As the fireflies giggle, giving all quite a fright.

Tulips play poker, with leaves as their stakes,
While pansies do gossip, make no mistakes.
The fragrant concoction of laughter and cheer,
Keeps all the garden folks drawing near.

As stars blink above, they join in the jest,
Casting shadows of bunnies, just trying to rest.
With each fragrant promise, a chuckle shall swell,
In this humorous twilight, all's perfectly well!

Colors of Serendipity

In hues of delight, colors clash and collide,
Yellow meets purple, with nowhere to hide.
The zinnias giggle, having quite the affair,
While tulips toss paint like a wild artist's flair.

Cacti don capes, feeling bold and so spry,
Lamenting their prickles, still eager to fly.
Daffodils bop, in their sunny best dress,
All sprouting a dance, who could ever guess?

Each bloom is a jest, a riot of cheer,
Petals in laughter, from far and from near.
The garden's a canvas, of humor and light,
With every new blossom, comes a giggle, all right!

So let colors clash, in a playful parade,
With nature's wild sense of humor displayed.
In the midst of the chaos, what joy to behold,
Life's vibrant palette, a spectacle bold!

Beneath the Canopy of Hope

Beneath leafy giants, the laughter flows free,
Squirrels juggle acorns, what a sight to see!
Rabbits deliver, the very best puns,
While dandelions issue their collective runs.

Sunbeams are ticklish, playing peek-a-boo,
As shadows grow longer, can you feel it too?
With a flutter of wings, the bluebirds croon,
While turtles tap dance, to a friendly tune.

Amidst ferns in the shade, a party unfolds,
With whispers of laughter, more precious than gold.
Lily pads bobbing in their joyous delight,
As frogs join the chorus, through day and through night.

In this leafy retreat, with giggles galore,
The canopy whispers of laughter and lore.
With every soft rustle, a chuckle prevails,
Beneath the bright branches, humor never fails!

A Spray of Wildflowers

In a patch of bright daisies, so spry,
A bumblebee danced, oh my, oh my!
He tripped on a petal, fell on his face,
   Then buzzed with style, full of grace.

The tulips were gossiping, quite the scene,
They whispered of weeds being so mean.
'Have you seen those thorns, such a rude lot?'
   Giggling, they sighed, 'Oh, what a plot!'

A ladybug crashed with a splash on a lily,
   Shouted, 'It's fine! I'm just feeling silly!'
She twirled in the sunshine, yellow and bright,
Proclaiming, 'I've conquered this flower-filled fright!'

So here's to the blooms, with stories to tell,
Of ants on the march and beetles that fell.
In this wild, wacky place where the flowers all play,
   Life's a comic strip in bright hues each day!

The Breath of Nature

Once upon a breeze, leaves took flight,
Whispering secrets of day and night.
A squirrel in stripes wore a nutty grin,
Challenged a bird to a race: let's begin!

The sunbeams giggled, lighting the glade,
While spiders spun webs for their grand parade.
A snort from a frog, as he leapt with a splash,
Chased away butterflies in a frantic dash.

Old oak trees chuckled, their branches so grand,
As kids in the meadow made castles of sand.
With each raucous laugh, the flowers would sway,
Nature's own chorus in exuberant play!

So when you might stroll where the wild things roam,
Listen for laughter; it feels like home.
For the breath of this place is a song, don't you see?
A riot of joy wrapped in greenery!

Petals on the Breeze

Petals afloat like a quirky kite,
Danced in the air, what a silly sight!
A wind gusted through, like a giggling child,
Knocking over sunflowers, oh how they smiled!

Grass had a party, all blades dressed up,
Joked with a pebble that rolled like a pup.
'We're better than rocks!' a tiny sprout cheered,
But the pebble just laughed, 'I'm well-rounded, dear!'

The daisies were swaying, they knew the score,
Hosting a bash, who could ask for more?
With ants tapping rhythms, the flora did groove,
Spreading good vibes, they were in the mood!

So let's join the fun, without any stress,
Where petals on breezes bring happiness.
In this rollicking realm where the critters all thrive,
Nature's a party, so come on, feel alive!

Moments in Full Bloom

In a patch of zinnias, laughter was loud,
A prickly old cactus gave a blooming crowd.
'Who needs a hug when you've got a flower?'
Chortled a dandelion, sprouting with power!

The rose tried a joke, with petals so bright,
'Why did the bee get stuck in a fright?'
'He wore the wrong cologne, far too sweet for his buzz!'
And all of the blossoms erupted like fuzz!

Pansies were planning their comedy show,
With punchlines as colorful as they could throw.
A sunflower beamed, its face to the sun,
'We're just getting started; oh, this will be fun!'

So cherish the blooms, their silliness too,
In moments of laughter, they touch hearts anew.
Amidst all the giggles and glee that they bring,
Nature's own circus, let the blossoms all sing!

Nature's Bounty Unveiled

In the plot where veggies play,
Carrots dance and peas display.
Tomatoes giggle, red and round,
While radishes bounce from the ground.

Zucchini wears a floppy hat,
Complaining about the garden cat.
Cucumbers slide down with a laugh,
While lettuce ponders its math craft.

Sunflowers tower, heads held high,
Trying to catch a passing fly.
Bumblebees hum a silly tune,
As daisies harmonize with the moon.

In this plot of leafy glee,
Nature's wonders sing with glee.
What a riot, this growing spree,
In the soil, we're all carefree!

Petals of Promise

In the morning, petals chat,
Roses gossip, 'Who's that brat?'
While daisies giggle and tease,
They whisper secrets on the breeze.

Tulips strut in rainbow hue,
Fashion statements, oh so true!
Violets chuckle, soft and shy,
Waving at passersby who cry.

Butterflies throw a costume ball,
With every flower having a call.
They flutter in their quirky clothes,
While sunflowers pose with their bows.

Every petal tells a joke,
In this place, joy's no hoax.
Laughter blooms in colors bright,
Chasing shadows away from sight.

Elysian Embrace

The trees are dancing, swaying wide,
Leaves flutter as if they've got pride.
Squirrels leap from branch to branch,
In this place, nothing's a chance.

Buttercups hold a shoe drop contest,
While bumblebees live for their quests.
Grasshoppers play a game of tag,
With every jump, they never lag.

Frogs in hats sing croaky tunes,
Under a sky with cheeky moons.
Rabbits giggle, munching away,
At the antics of their playful day.

In harmony, each creature finds,
Joy in the dance of nature's kinds.
With laughter ringing through the trees,
This embrace is filled with ease.

The Blooming Heart

In the patch where hearts bloom bright,
Cacti tell jokes, poke fun, delight.
Petunias prance with nimble feet,
While daisies offer snacks to eat.

A gopher with a top hat sings,
While butterflies flit and do rings.
Worms wiggle with their secret score,
Creating tunes that shake the floor.

Sweet peas giggle with joy so spry,
As hummingbirds zip, oh my, oh my!
Sunflowers wink with a knowing smile,
Inviting all to stay a while.

Here, the heart finds a playful role,
In every petal, in every hole.
Blooming laughter, bright and fair,
Filling the air with love to share.